Trish's Ship

by Ron Hart
illustrated by Jan Pyk

Core Decodable 40

McGraw Hill Education

Bothell, WA • Chicago, IL • Columbus, OH • New York, NY

MHEonline.com

Send all inquiries to:
McGraw-Hill Education
8787 Orion Place
Columbus, OH 43240

ISBN: 978-0-02-145474-7
MHID: 0-02-145474-4

Printed in Canada.

9 10 11 12 KOD 24

Trish fishes.

Trish picks up shells.

Can Trish spot a ship?

Is it stashed in the shed?

It is! A ship is stashed in the shed.

Trish has a plan. Trish gets Mom.
Trish brushes the sand.

Trish calls the ship "The Shellfish."

Trish's ship splashes in the sun.